THE SUCKERS GUIDE

A Journey into the Soft Centre of the Sweet Shop

JON STROUD

THE SUCKER'S GUIDE

Summersdale Publishers Ltd
46 West Street
Chichester
West Sussex
PO19 1RP
UK

www.summersdale.com

Printed and bound by Imago

ISBN: 978-1-84024-709-1

Extract from Roy Fuller's poem 'Necrophagy' is copyright and used with the kindest permission of John Fuller.

Disclaimer
Every effort has been taken to ensure that the information in this book is accurate and current at the time of publication. Readers, particularly those with specific dietary requirements or allergies, should always check that the sweets they are purchasing comply with their needs as different manufacturers' recipes and production methods could vary. Remember, sweets may cause tooth decay – be sure to visit your dentist regularly.

ABOUT THE
AUTHOR

Jon Stroud spent his formative years walking home from school clutching a small paper bag packed full of Cola Bottles, Flying Saucers and Pink Shrimps. He now lives in a small village in the Gloucestershire Cotswolds where he writes books, takes photographs and still eats too many sweets. His dentist is Mr Ellis.

INTRODUCTION

Some eat the jelly baby whole but most
Dismember it at leisure
For headless, there's no doubt it gives
A reasonable measure
Of unexampled pleasure

From the poem 'Necrophagy' by Roy Fuller

All of us love to munch on a sweet from time to time and everyone has a personal favourite. Like familiar songs heard on the radio, they can instantly transport us back to our youth with memories of summer holidays, cinema trips and long walks home from school clutching a small paper bag packed full to bursting with carefully selected sugary treats.

There can be few experiences more enjoyable or rewarding than a trip to the local sweet shop: shelves stacked high with glass jars, each filled to the brim with a multitude of technicoloured candies; the sugary aroma that hangs in the air; the distinctive rattle as customers' selections are weighed out; the open boxes of tantalising penny confections – Cola Bottles, Flying Saucers, White Mice and Black Jacks; the uncontrollable temptation to try every sweet in the shop.

After many years of resistance it is that very temptation that has got the better of me. I have tried every sweet in the shop and the result is this: *The Sucker's Guide: A Journey into the Soft Centre of the Sweet Shop*. With so much confectionery on offer, paring it down to this small selection meant making some difficult choices – a task made somewhat easier thanks to the assistance of Sue King and Julie Hawker of Coco in Nailsworth. I am sure there are some people whose favourites have been omitted whilst others will find that some of the choices make them screw up their face in distaste. What is certain is that it includes some of the most popular, the most nostalgic and, in some cases, the most unusual sweets in the shop.

Turn on, tune in, pig out.

USING THE GUIDE

The Sucker's Guide has been created to ensure that your personal journey into the soft centre of the sweet shop is a safe and enjoyable one. To help you on your way I have painstakingly researched each confection.

Each entry provides:

- A useful and informative description to assist your sweet purchasing decisions
- A fact about the confection
- Suggestions for alternative confections
- Accurate specifications, including the essential Hero-2-Zero rating detailing how long each sweet can be expected to last (or how long the flavour lasts for gums)

Key to the icons

Each entry also includes easy-to-recognise icons which show you at a glance the confection's key features. Below is an explanation of what each of these means.

Dietary

 Vegetarian

 Vegetarian Option Available

 Gluten Free

 Sugar Free Option Available

 Halal Option Available

Packaging

 Penny – those traditionally bought individually

 Jar – those weighed out, sadly no longer by the quarter

 Packet – those sold in their own self-contained packet, tube or box

Texture

 Jelly

 Bubbly

 Hard

 Soft

Flavour

 Sweet

 Sour

 Liquorice or Aniseed

 Mint

 Chocolate

 White Chocolate

 Herbal

 Fizzy

ANGLO BUBBLY

Length:
22 mm

Width:
20 mm

Depth:
9 mm

Weight:
9 g

Hero-2-Zero:
3 min 45 sec

Unfortunately, my bubble-blowing talents are not in a sufficiently high state of tune to tell you whether Anglo Bubbly is the ultimate gum for making large pink bubbles. However, what I can tell you is that, in my humble opinion, it is by far the best tasting.

Once removed from its brightly coloured wrapper and popped in the mouth, the small pink medallion soon becomes wonderfully soft, succulent and full of flavour, although the actual composition of the flavour remains open for debate. Sadly, as with the vast majority of gums, this flavour is not particularly long lasting. Vigorous chewing will soon leave you with nothing more than a listless and rather sickly looking globule devoid of taste and texture and create an entirely new dilemma of what to do with the lifeless residue – any schoolchild worth their salt will know that swallowing gum will result in a slow, painful and untimely death.

Whilst this is not entirely true it has, over many years, proved sufficient incentive for children to find ever more inventive methods of gum disposal. How many of us at some point in our youth attempted to leave a classroom only to find that one of our knees had inadvertently become welded to the underside of a desk?

FACT Frank H. Fleer invented bubblegum in 1906 – it is traditionally pink because no other colouring was in stock when he made it!

WHY NOT TRY...

Bazooka – with a free comic too!

Gold Nuggets – a bubbly bag of fun

ANISEED BALL

Diameter:
15 mm

Weight:
3 g

Hero-2-Zero:
9 min 27 sec

Could there be any sweet more evocative of childhood misdemeanours than the Aniseed Ball? Alongside a magnifying glass, a pocket knife (in the days when boys carried a blade for whittling sticks rather than each other), several marbles and a random length of string, this ball bearing of a confection was once regarded as de rigueur pocket content for any self-respecting young tyke in shorts and a school cap.

Away from its scholarly connections, the *boule d'anis* is truly a thing of beauty. Whilst many sweets arrive in the bag knocked, chipped or squashed beyond recognition, these burgundy orbs (constructed, it seems, to a near military specification) invariably survive intact. Their curious indestructibility leads one to consider that should the planet ever succumb to a global catastrophe, in all probability the only survivors would be aniseed balls and cockroaches.

To consume, the aniseed ball holds few surprises – that is unless the taste of the *Pimpinella anisum* is foreign to your palette. This is a sweet not to be crunched. Indeed, doing so could well result in a hefty dental repair bill. No, the trick is to allow the sphere to roll effortlessly around the mouth as first you strip away the outer coloured shell and then you work your way through the porcelain interior (occasionally allowing yourself a satisfying rattle on the back of your teeth). Only after considerable labour is the ultimate reward of a rape-seed centre finally revealed.

FACT

Leaves your whole mouth a satisfying shade of purple.

WHY NOT TRY...

Army & Navy – with a little bit of liquorice thrown in

Poor Bens – the gummy alternative

ARMY & NAVY

Length:
30 mm

Width:
17 mm

Depth:
10 mm

Weight:
6 g

Hero-2-Zero:
6 min 41 sec

For many a year I considered the Army & Navy to be something of an enigma – not through a lack of understanding of our nation's fighting forces but, rather, because there existed a rather curious sugar-coated inky black sweet of the same name and I knew nothing of its hidden delights.

The reason for my limited or, in fact, non-existent knowledge of this confection soon became obvious – I didn't possess the Army & Navy gene. This is something that is handed down from generation to generation like a fine engraved pocket watch, ancestral portrait or family funeral business. Quite simply, if a family member hasn't initiated you into the mysterious world of the paregoric then you probably have never sampled its delights.

Originally known as the Army & Navy Paregoric, legend tells how this aniseed and liquorice morsel was developed for the War Office and the Admiralty during World War One as an aid for keeping officers' voices clear and true above the din of battle in the trenches of Europe and on the high seas – perish the thought that some poor serviceman could get cut to ribbons for King and Country just because his captain's vocal cords were weakened through consuming an incorrect confection!

Has it stood the test of time? Without a doubt, yes! Its traditional shape fits perfectly on the tongue, and whilst its sugar coating is pleasingly abrasive at first, it gives way to a silky smooth lozenge beneath, revealing the soothing medicinal properties of the Army & Navy sweet itself.

FACT

EU Regulations mean that the Paregoric part of the name can no longer be used.

WHY NOT TRY...

Cough Candy – a liquorice-free option

Grays Herbals – if you're not a fan of aniseed

BARLEY SUGAR

Length:
25 mm

Width:
25 mm

Depth:
13 mm

Weight:
8 g

Hero-2-Zero:
5 min 11 sec

A true old-time confection, the humble Barley Sugar has roots that can be traced back as far as the seventeenth century when it was first produced by boiling down refined cane sugar with barley water. Lauded by Mrs Beeton and incredibly simple to make, tons of the stuff has been brewed in grandmothers' kitchens across the land ever since – the resulting hard slabs being cut into strips and then twisted by hand into delightfully spiralling sticks that bring gleeful looks to the faces of countless children. Be warned – sugar at boiling point can be a vicious substance with a mind of its own.

Golden in colour and surprisingly warming to the taste buds, the modern day descendent of this traditional boiled sweet is a far safer concern and, like a fine painting by Constable or Turner, evokes memories of warm summer evenings, bringing in the harvest and lining oneself up for a cooling pint of draught cider at the local village establishment – quite a remarkable achievement for any sweet if you grew up in a provincial commuter-belt town as I did.

In a world where so many products are now burdened with unnecessary gimmicks, the Barley Sugar still stands proud, simple and steeped in tradition. It is a true confectionery classic.

FACT Want to know more? Visit the Moret Nuns Barley Sugar Museum in Moret-sur-Loing, France.

WHY NOT TRY...

Mint Humbugs – another traditional favourite

Cough Candy – a classic soother

BAZOOKA

Length: **30 mm**	
Width: **20 mm**	
Depth: **5 mm**	
Weight: **5 g**	
Hero-2-Zero: **1 min 52 sec**	

If, in your youth, blowing rather than sucking was your thing, no self-respecting bag of penny sweets was complete without a Bazooka Bubble Gum. This statutory requirement was, however, not just about the gum. Whilst it is said the luscious and juicy Anglo Bubbly arguably provides a superior bubble blowing experience, the Bazooka offered something truly unique – a miniature comic strip about the eponymous character Bazooka Joe concealed beneath its patriotic red, white and blue wrapper. Unintelligible, unfunny and immensely confusing it may have been, but it was free – and when you are eight years old free booty means everything and more.

In all of the years since it was launched just after World War Two, what Bazooka Gum actually tastes of nobody seems to be quite sure. In more recent times vaguely discernible flavours such as Strawberry Shake, Cherry Berry, Watermelon Whirl and Grape Rage have all been introduced for the delectation of American gum-guzzlers. It is, however, Original that remains to this day the best-seller by far. I have seen strawberries, cherries, watermelons and even grapes for sale in my local supermarket but have never come across a punnet of Originals. Until that moment arrives, the secret behind the oral delight of the Bazooka will remain one of life's mysteries.

FACT

The Bazooka Joe cartoon strips were first introduced in 1953 – since then there have been over 700 different ones. In the United States the strips can be collected and then exchanged for Bazooka branded goodies!

WHY NOT TRY...

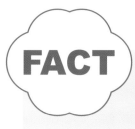

Anglo Bubbly – the best of British

Gold Nuggets – worth it for the free bag

BLACK JACK

Length: **24 mm**	
Width: **15 mm**	
Depth: **6 mm**	
Weight: **3 g**	
Hero-2-Zero: **1 min 8 sec**	

Whilst undoubtedly a member of the penny sweet royal family, the Barratt's Black Jack is far from being everyone's cup of tea. The reason? Aniseed. To the initiated, this wonderful flavour is a true delight. Strong, but far from overpowering, it acts as a perfect antidote to other super-sweet confections.

As a soft chew the Black Jack does not, under normal circumstances, lend itself to any specialist techniques in consumption. It is, however, worth noting that, when very cold (for example, after having been left overnight in a car), it may become hard and brittle – a condition easily remedied by simply holding the unwrapped sweet in your mouth for ten to fifteen seconds before proceeding as usual.

Although the humble Black Jack has been a staple of the British sweet shop since it was introduced in the early 1920s by Trebor, it has, in more recent years, undergone a makeover. Dressed now in a black, white and red wrapper of swirling abstract design, it spent the majority of its years in a simple black and white greaseproof wrapper featuring a classic golliwog. Like the smiling fellow who used to grace the jars of Robertson's jam, this icon of British confection has now been consigned to the history books.

FACT There is an original Golly Black Jack wrapper on display in London's Victoria and Albert Museum.

WHY NOT TRY...

Fruit Salad – the Black Jack's fruity cousin

Spogs – aniseed in a bobbly package

BLACKCURRANT AND LIQUORICE

Length:
30 mm

Width:
20 mm

Depth:
13 mm

Weight:
9 g

Hero-2-Zero:
8 min 14 sec

Deliciously warm and sticky, the Blackcurrant and Liquorice has become a personal firm favourite. Almost regal in appearance, its purple and gold wrapper strips away to reveal a boiled sweet of near gem-like quality that, when held against the light, dares you to pop it in your mouth and indulge in its magnificent taste explosion.

After a period of prolonged sucking, the flavoursome outer-shell (whose taste is reminiscent of an autumn fruits crumble) gives way to a wonderfully sweet liquorice toffee centre. Without having tasted a Blackcurrant and Liquorice it would be difficult to imagine how two such seemingly opposing flavours could possibly be successfully combined, but the fact remains that the resulting concoction has a flavour that even Gordon Ramsay would be proud of.

   Aware of the sweet and soft centre within, it may be a temptation to crunch away from the outset. Whilst there is obviously nothing wrong with this full-on approach, to my mind the enjoyment this confection offers comes in part from the knowing anticipation that, at any moment, the flavour will change entirely from fruit to root, effectively giving you two sweet sensations for the price of one.

FACT You can buy another version that is hard all the way through.

WHY NOT TRY...

Chocolate Limes – sharp but sweet

Poor Bens – chewy with a difference

BONBON

Diameter:
20 mm

Weight:
6 g

Hero-2-Zero:
6 min 02 sec

The word 'bonbon' means different things to different people. For some it's an ice cream dessert, for others it is a sugar-coated almond. Some nations, notably the French and the Germans, even use bonbon as a generic term for all sweets and candy. Who does not remember those long strips of sweets you bought on the school day trip to Boulogne-sur-Mer, alongside the bangers, naughty playing cards and Pas-de-Calais key fobs?

All these are perfectly valid uses of the term but, should you request a Bonbon in a traditional British sweet shop you will be offered something altogether different – a chewy-centred confection dusted in icing sugar. Although my personal preference is the Toffee Bonbon (white in colour with a wonderful cream toffee core), many other flavoured varieties are available to suit the individual palate. Strawberry and Lemon are perhaps the most common alternative, joined happily by more exotic varieties such as apple, chocolate or even Vimto, with its own curious combination of grape, raspberry and blackcurrant.

The Bonbon is a most satisfying confection to consume. Its sugary coating primes the tongue and encourages you to roll its spherical form about the mouth until all that remains is the toffee centre. The option now, to either suck or chew, is entirely down to choice – I prefer to continue sucking as this reduces the risk of unintentionally dislodging a dental filling.

FACT In Edgar Allan Poe's 1832 short story 'Bon-Bon' the devil has a predilection for eating the souls of philosophers.

WHY NOT TRY...

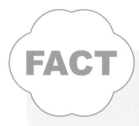

Grays Teacakes – toffee wrapped in coconut

Highland Toffee Bar – soft and smooth

BOYNES SUGAR MICE

Length:
140 mm
(inc tail)

Width:
29 mm

Depth:
18 mm

Weight:
25 g

Hero-2-Zero:
4 min 25 sec

Wow! What an amazing sweet this is! Truly in the premier league of British confection, the Boynes Sugar Mouse has graced sweet shops across the land since the company was founded in 1919. The concept of making sugary animals can be traced back as far as Roman times with a peak in popularity during the sixteenth century. In fact, legend has it that the origin of the Sugar Mouse itself can be traced back to when Tudor children were given real mice dipped in sugar to keep them quiet whilst their parents were presumably busy discovering potatoes and fending off Spanish invasions.

Whether that's true or not, the modern day Sugar Mouse is an altogether more palatable concern but even in my lifetime it has undergone a plethora of changes – all for the good you will be pleased to hear. Gone is the tooth-breaking hard confection of old. Now we are treated to a sugary rodent that is smooth, soft and sweet, and made using all natural colours and flavourings. A health food it may not be, but a healthier food it has clearly become.

One thing, however, remains delightfully unchanged – perfect for dangling the little fellow in your mouth, every single mouse still has a real cotton string tail (inedible, of course) painstakingly attached by hand. With over a million Boynes Sugar Mice produced every year, that's a lot of tail sticking!

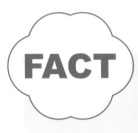

FACT Boynes Sugar Mice make an appearance in the film of J. K. Rowling's *Harry Potter and the Order of the Phoenix.*

WHY NOT TRY...

Chocolate Mice – a chocolatey alternative

White Mice – the smooth albino

CANDY LETTERS

Length:
15 mm

Width:
15 mm

Depth:
5 mm

Weight:
1.3 g

Hero-2-Zero:
15 sec
(per letter)

Educational eating? Whilst I am sure a dietician would have some choice words on the subject, there is no doubt that Candy Letters are a great way of encouraging youngsters to learn how to spell. But don't get too carried away at the prospect of these pastel-shaded confections being the answer to every child's primary education needs: unless your local sweet shop is prepared to show a great deal of patience and consideration in permitting you to make your own selection of letters then the chances of your child being able to construct any meaningful words (let alone sentences) are next to zero. That is, unless your offspring happens to be a Boggle Grand Master.

I am sure there are many who would disagree but, for me, the Candy Letter is not particularly exciting to eat. Over-sweet and rather chalky, it rates as a poor cousin to the Fizzer, Refresher or even the Candy Necklace.

FACT

Written in Candy Letters, this sentence would weigh about sixty grams.

WHY NOT TRY...

Love Hearts – you can't help but love these

Candy Necklace – the wearable treat

CANDY NECKLACE

Length:
320 mm

Width:
10 mm

Depth:
5 mm

Weight:
23 g

Hero-2-Zero:
**20 sec
(per bead)**

What is it that would prompt an otherwise sensible adult woman to don a Candy Necklace in place of designer jewellery? That is the clever thing about this truly original confection – it has to be worn. No ifs, no buts. What, after all, would be the point of an edible necklace if it remained in your hand rather than round your neck?

Whereas some candy novelties can be somewhat devoid of flavour, the Candy Necklace commends itself by being rather tasty. Care, however, must be taken when biting away the tiny multicoloured rings. It is all too easy to pull away at the elastic thong only to end up firing a small sweet projectile across the room, leaving your sweet tooth unsatisfied.

If you have a desire to accessorise further, then a rather smart Candy Watch is also available whilst, for those looking for an altogether more entertaining sweet solution, there are retailers who will be more than happy to provide you with matching candy underwear or even a set of edible cuffs!

FACT The Candy Necklace is considered such a design icon you can now buy one made of real gold and silver candy beads. Whilst attractive to look at, eating these precious metals is not advised!

WHY NOT TRY...

Candy Letters – eat your way through the alphabet

Swizzels Double Lolly – same taste, bigger package

CANDY STICKS

Length:
53 mm

Width:
5 mm

Depth:
5 mm

Weight:
2 g (each)

Hero-2-Zero:
47 sec (each)

It is astonishing to think that just a few short years ago it was considered completely appropriate for an eight year old to be given a packet of replica cigarettes to suck upon – just the thing to go with a can of Top Deck lager shandy! But that is just the way it was. Candy Sticks, as they are now monikered, used to be known as Sweet Cigarettes and came complete with a glowing tip just so you knew which end was to be sucked first.

Thanks to the backlash against smoking the red tip has disappeared forever, leaving us with a rather pallid rod that looks like a spare part from an Airfix model kit and tastes little better. The Candy Stick is, however, not wholly without merit. Its joy comes not from the flavour (which purports to be pineapple) but from the fun you can have working the end into a fine point with your tongue.

Although there was no avoiding the fact that Candy Sticks possessed an undeniable link with tobacco, the blow was somewhat softened by the innocent way they were packaged. There was no such soft sell with their chocolatey cousin. For a start, the packaging perfectly replicates the traditional soft pack used by many cigarette brands right down to the foil inner wrapping and paper seal. But, for all of its questionable morality, there is no denying that the Chocolate Cigarette is a tasty confection. Often, chocolate of this type (the mass-produced continental variety) proves far too sweet; however, in a small, carefully controlled dose such as this, it proves more than palatable. Chocolate Lights, anybody?

If, when rummaging through your childhood possessions, you happen across one of the original Sweet Cigarette boxes do not under any circumstances be tempted to throw it out! Highly collectable, they frequently reach surprisingly high prices on Internet auction sites.

FACT Superman used to be seen in anti-smoking campaigns on TV fighting Nick O'Teen – now he appears on some boxes of Candy Sticks!

WHY NOT TRY...

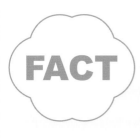

Chocolate Cigarettes – if you prefer cocoa

Spanish Gold – the original sweet tobacco

CATHERINE WHEEL

Diameter:
45 mm
(coiled)

Depth:
8 mm

Weight:
16 g

Hero-2-Zero:
3 min 15 sec

On the face of it, Catherine Wheels are pretty straightforward things. After all, it does not take a genius to recognise that it is nothing more than a thin, soft liquorice strip coiled around a yummy Spog. But such a simple description fails to convey the joy that this spiralling confection offers.

Sweets are not just there for eating: they are playthings to be enjoyed and admired. Think to yourself (assuming that the taste of liquorice does not leave you green in the face) how much pure pleasure can be derived from gradually unreeling the liquorice from around the Spog and, in turn, reeling it back up around your tongue. And then there is the Spog itself – the aniseed reward for all of your liquoricy toil. Could there be a better prize for your efforts?

The Catherine Wheel is a marvel of design – 400 mm of liquorice presented in a compact, self-dispensing format. Is black the new green? Ferdinand Porsche would be proud!

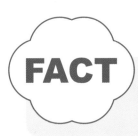

FACT The Liquorice Catherine Wheel is probably named after the firework but the original Catherine wheel was a medieval instrument of torture!

WHY NOT TRY...

Spogs – how could you not?

Liquorice Allsorts – everyone likes an Allsort

CHOCOLATE-COATED BANANA

Length:
105 mm

Width:
30 mm

Depth:
15 mm

Weight:
29 g

Hero-2-Zero:
1 min 18 sec

I like bananas – not only for their taste but also for the outstanding way in which Mother Nature has created the perfect snack-food complete with its own biodegradable wrapper. But then there is also something wonderful about the way the world can take a perfectly healthy natural product such as this and reinvent it as a sugary, calorie-packed confection. We should be very thankful it did.

There are two types of banana-shaped sweet available to satisfy the monkey in all of us. The first is the rather firm and chewy foam banana (the small, yellow cousin of the classic Pink Shrimp that is also supplied naked and chocolate free). These, whilst not at all unpleasant, can prove quite hard work as their centre requires a considerable amount of chewing. Eat too many, and the taste soon becomes rather sickly.

The alternative is a far more luxurious option – over ten centimetres of the softest, stickiest, banana-flavoured marshmallow coated in a tantalisingly thin layer of high quality dark chocolate that cracks effortlessly when bitten. The balance of banana and chocolate is perfection itself.

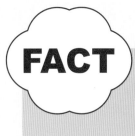

FACT The artificial banana flavouring used in sweets, the delightfully named ester isoamyl acetate ($CH_3COOC_5H_{11}$), is potent stuff! Just a couple of molecules can make anything taste bananary!

WHY NOT TRY...

Fried Eggs – more foamy fun

Pink Shrimps – sweet little sea creatures

CHOCOLATE LIME

Length:
30 mm

Width:
16 mm

Depth:
16 mm

Weight:
8 g

Hero-2-Zero:
6 min 33 sec

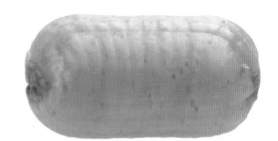

Chocolate and lime – whoever first came up with the idea of combining these two great flavours is to be congratulated. From the moment it is unwrapped this sweet is a pleasure to behold. Its colouring is that of a sun-kissed meadow – its just-visible chocolate centre encouraging you to indulge in its delights without further ado.

As with its cousin, the Blackcurrant and Liquorice, the skill of the Chocolate Lime comes in the way in which it is consumed. No early crunching here, please. Instead, take your time to enjoy the citrus outer shell with its hint of sharpness that appeals to those who would normally consider a boiled confection too sweet. Your reward for refraining from the use of your molars is the gentle and sustained release of the chocolatey core throughout the eating process. Crunch at your own peril for, if you do so, the chocolate treat will be lost in an instant.

Whilst a tasty pleasure for any child, there is something curiously grown up about the Chocolate Lime. It is one of those sweets that seem to mark the passing of time – like the moment you stopped listening to Radio 1 in the morning and finally tuned in to the dulcet tones of Terry Wogan and Ken Bruce on Radio 2. Chocolate Limes – the nation's favourite?

FACT In the nineteenth century, British sailors were issued with a daily ration of lime to combat scurvy.

WHY NOT TRY...

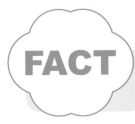

Rhubarb & Custard – sweet and sour perfection

Sherbet Lemons – effervescent pondering power

CHOCOLATE MICE

Length:	40 mm
Width:	18 mm
Depth:	10 mm
Weight:	4 g
Hero-2-Zero:	24 sec

Yet another staple of the ten-penny bag of sweets is the Chocolate Mouse. Alongside the Cola Bottle, Black Jack and Fruit Salad it was a frontline choice in the after-school corner-shop melee.

Of the two varieties available, the albino version is by far the most appetising – its rich and creamy texture comes close to rivalling Fish & Chips at the head of the white chocolate league. In a bizarre contrast, the darker milk chocolate flavoured Mouse definitely falls short of the mark. Chocolate can be a magnificent thing. The Belgians, the Swiss and even the British make some wonderful examples which are smooth, velvety and thoroughly delightful. Why, then, is the stuff that goes into making these little brown rodents so disappointing?

Little skill or instruction is needed regarding their consumption. For most people the pop-it-in-in-one technique would seem the most obvious solution, but to suggest that this is the only way would be wholly misleading. After all, who among us has not taken secret delight in biting the head off a Chocolate Mouse?

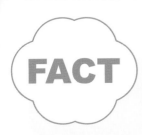
WHY NOT TRY...

Boynes Sugar Mice – the sugary original

Fish & Chips – white chocolate at its absolute best

CHUPA CHUPS

Length:
90 mm
(inc stick)

Width:
25 mm

Depth:
25 mm

Weight:
13 g

Hero-2-Zero:
6 min 26 sec

First things first – and this may come as a shock and turn your childhood memories upside down – it is pronounced 'choo-pah choops'. Honestly!

Nobody is quite sure when the lollipop was first invented. Even the origin of the word seems to be an enigma: some references suggest that it was a term coined in 1931 by the American confectioner George Smith in honour of his favourite horse, Lolly Pop, whilst others believe that it dates back to Dickensian London. Whichever is correct, the origin of the sweet itself can be traced back much further, as it has been shown that both the Ancient Egyptians and Chinese produced sticky confections served on sticks.

The world's best-loved lollipop, as its Spanish manufacturers like to call it, was created in 1958 by entrepreneur Enric Bernat – the grandson of Spain's first confectioner, Josep Bernat. Inevitably, the intervening years have witnessed a great deal of change for this popular treat. Plastic has replaced the original wooden sticks, more flavours have been introduced to suit contemporary tastes and new recipes have been developed to entice the diet-conscious sweet addict (the Chupa Chups Cremosa is sugar free and contains only 33 calories).

One thing has not changed. After fifty years, they still taste amazing. There are countless types of lollipop available across the land but few, if any, could claim to be as delicious as the Iberian original. Faultless in size and shape (a near perfect sphere) it stimulates the taste buds from first suck to last without cracking, splitting or falling away from its stick. A true masterpiece!

FACT

The Chupa Chups logo was designed by surrealist artist Salvador Dali in 1969.

WHY NOT TRY...

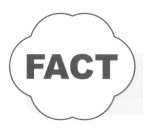

Traffic Light Lolly – the colour changing confection

Drumstick – chewy fun on a stick

CINDER TOFFEE

Length:
30 mm
(average)

Width:
30 mm
(average)

Depth:
20 mm
(average)

Weight:
6 g
(average)

Hero-2-Zero:
41 sec

Those from north of the border might know it as Puff Candy. To those across the Irish Sea (or, indeed, across the Atlantic) it is probably Sponge Toffee. If you are clinging on to the other side of the planet in Australia or New Zealand, then it is most likely that Hokey Pokey will ring a bell. For the rest of us it is either Honeycomb or, more correctly, Cinder Toffee – that wonderfully light and airy sugar-laden treat that rekindles memories of funfairs, bonfire nights and seaside holidays.

If your only experience of this has been a brittle concoction hidden beneath a thin layer of chocolate in a Crunchie bar then think again – real Cinder Toffee is something quite different. It should be light and crisp to the touch but, once in your mouth, should melt away to become gorgeously sticky and chewy with the most sublime rich caramel taste possible. One piece is, quite simply, never enough for anybody.

One of the real beauties of Cinder Toffee is that, unlike almost every other confectionery on the market, it is infinitely simple to make at home. Nothing more than sugar, golden syrup, butter and, of course, the tiniest splash of malt vinegar and bicarbonate of soda to make the mixture fizz and foam. Find yourself a recipe and get cooking – but do let it cool before you eat the lot!

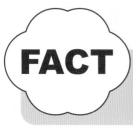

FACT

From Mrs Beeton to Delia Smith, many of the nation's greatest cooks have been big fans of Cinder Toffee and have written their own recipes for the stuff!

WHY NOT TRY...

Grays Teacakes – soft and syrupy

Icy Cups – another taste of the fairground

COCONUT

MUSHROOM

Length:
25 mm

Width:
25 mm

Depth:
25 mm

Weight:
7 g

Hero-2-Zero:
1 min 41 sec

Often, when a sweet takes on an unconventional design, the result is a victory for form over function. Quite frankly, some of the most appetising sweets by appearance can be the most disappointing when it comes to the act of consumption. Not so the Coconut Mushroom.

The idea of marrying a hard candy stalk with a sticky chocolate and coconut fondant cap is one of the great intellectual achievements of the twentieth century and on a par with the work of Einstein and Oppenheimer. However, if you are tempted to partake in this sweet fungal delight, take care in your choice of supplier for only the best mushrooms have their caps truly saturated with desiccated coconut – lesser examples bear only a token quantity stuck to the outside of what is invariably inferior marshmallow.

There are no rules or regulations for consumption although there is an obvious temptation to dissect the sweet in your hand and then treat each of the halves as an individual treat.

For many years the Coconut Mushroom's unique shape set it aside from the contents of other sweet shop jars, but in recent years a fruity doppelgänger has appeared in the form of the Foam Mushroom. Pink, yellow and orange in colour, these chewy sweets are most definitely a tasty treat in their own right, but to compare them with the coconut original would be like comparing John Noakes with Gethin Jones – both have presented Blue Peter but you'll only remember one of them 20 years from now.

FACT

Don't be fooled if you see Coconut Mushroom on the menu in a Thai restaurant – it's probably the soup.

WHY NOT TRY...

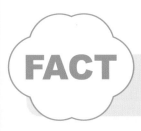

Spanish Gold – moreish in the extreme

Toasted Teacakes – soft, succulent coconut

COLA BOTTLE

Length:
32 mm

Width:
16 mm

Depth:
8 mm

Weight:
12 g

Hero-2-Zero:
**15 sec
(chewed)
3 min 21 sec
(sucked)**

The Jelly Cola Bottle without a doubt represents the benchmark in penny sweets. Although it is not everybody's favourite gummy morsel, there surely has never been a clammy child's hand that has not grasped a paper bag packed full with these little bottles of sugary goodness.

From the moment a Cola Bottle (it is normal practice in sweet shop parlance to drop the word 'Jelly' in favour of this more colloquial term) enters the mouth, your taste buds are enveloped in the exquisite flavour of a can of flat coke. Bliss! The delight of the Cola Bottle does not, however, finish there. Fitting conveniently over or under the tongue, when gently rolled in the mouth a standard example can last for several minutes, although the method de rigueur usually involves a sumptuous high speed chomp of about 15 seconds making this a true Hero-2-Zero speed merchant.

The Cola Bottle is available in a variety of shapes and sizes, from the 'mini' found in many variety mixes, through the standard 'Cola'-embossed favourite, to the oversized but oh-so-tasty Giant Cola Bottle. It should, however, not be confused with the similarly named Fizzy Cola Bottle which, although sharing the same basic cola taste, offers an entirely different edible experience. Could the Fizzy Cola Bottle be set to steal its jelly cousin's crown as the definitive penny sweet offering? Its enormous increase in popularity in recent years could easily lead one to believe so.

The changing taste of the nation has seen a marked rise in the reputation of sweets with a bit more bite – something that the latter day Fizzy Cola Bottle offers by the mouthful. Whilst early Fizzy Cola Bottles were little more than replicas of their smooth jelly relation encrusted with a smattering of sugar, in its current incarnation it offers a taste experience so sharp that it could cut paper. Only an extraordinarily strong individual could possibly resist pursing their lips when sampling one for the first time.

FACT Each day Haribo manufactures over 250,000 Cola Bottles!

WHY NOT TRY...

Fizzy Cola Bottles – the fizzy, sour alternative

Mojo Cola Chew – ideal for popping in your pocket

DRUMSTICK

Length:
46 mm

Width:
22 mm

Depth:
11 mm

Weight:
11 g

Hero-2-Zero:
4 min 19 sec

The Swizzels Matlow Drumstick is a bit of an enigma. Is it or is it not a true lollipop? Its packaging describes it as a 'chewy sweet lolly' but, to my mind, a lolly should be a confection where the sweet and the stick remain connected until the very final suck. By contrast, to fully enjoy a Drumstick in all its glory one must first strip the edible head clean of its inedible rolled paper stick – then, and only then, can it be chewed as intended.

Moans, groans and technicalities aside, the Drumstick is a prince amongst chews not least due to its impressive and excessive size and weight (for those of you who enjoy statistics: 1 x Drumstick = 3 x Fruit Salad). It also rates pretty highly in the taste department. Whilst raspberry and milk (yes milk!) might not normally be considered obvious bedfellows their combination in this case proves to be outstanding.

When first popping a Drumstick in your mouth it is easy to be fooled into thinking that the eating process will be an exhausting one, for this leviathan takes a little work to bring up to optimum temperature. However, once warmed with body heat the chew becomes soft and malleable and the experience becomes effortless.

FACT Drumsticks are wrapped by a special machine at a rate of 500 lollipops per minute.

WHY NOT TRY...

 **Fruit Salad – a miniature chewy classic**

 **Wham Bar – sweet and stretchy**

FISH & CHIPS

Fish/Chip

Length:
51/50 mm

Width:
32/20 mm

Depth:
10/10 mm

Weight:
9/9 g

Hero-2-Zero:
1 min 12 sec

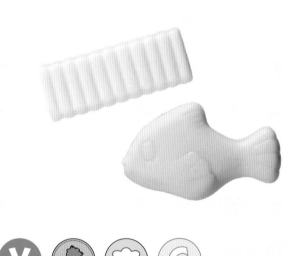

Yum, yum, yum! Can white chocolate get any better than that found in Fish & Chips? Smooth and creamy, this is one of life's sublime melt-in-your-mouth treats. Why Fish & Chips? I have absolutely no clue, but the idea of producing confections in the shape of animals is well documented and longstanding. Yes, I know the chip is not an animal, but I think the concept still holds a respectable degree of validity.

But which is better – the fish or the chip? Despite the fish appearing to be slightly larger, by weight there is no difference whatsoever. The defining factor, therefore, must be form. Is it the smooth, slippery fish or the traditionally crinkled chip that cuts the mustard? Although the fish allows you the opportunity to partake in the satisfying pastime of head biting (see Chocolate Mouse) the verdict, to my mind, must go in favour of the chip, its serrations providing ideally spaced, nibble-sized portions.

Fish and chips was once the most popular meal in Britain but, alas, it has been dethroned by the dreaded chicken tikka masala. Let's hope the yummy white chocolate Fish & Chips don't suffer the same fate to a gummy curry-shaped interloper.

FACT

In some countries white chocolate cannot be called chocolate at all due to the fact that it contains cocoa butter instead of cocoa solids.

WHY NOT TRY...

White Mice – try biting off the heads

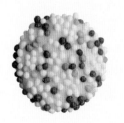

Jazzies (White Chocolate) – with added crunch

FIZZ WIZ

Length:
110 mm

Width:
65 mm

Depth:
5 mm

Weight:
10 g

Hero-2-Zero:
**5 min 33 sec
(per packet)**

How much fun is it possible to have with a packet of sweets and still remain on the right side of the law? Fizz Wiz, Space Dust, Pop Rocks – call it what you will: when popping candy arrived in the sweet shops in 1975 it became the must-have confection for any child who had imagined sitting behind the controls of an X-wing fighter on a mission to defeat the Death Star.

Once in the mouth, these little sugar-like crystals react in the most incredible fashion creating a veritable firework display of fizz on the tongue worthy (in the mind of an eight-year-old at least) of the very best Hollywood sci-fi blockbuster. Almost immediately a crackling sensation takes over your mouth with a THX quality soundtrack so crystal clear it feels as if it is being projected directly into your cerebral cortex, bypassing the aural receptors entirely.

For some time rumours circulated claiming that if you were to consume a combination of Space Dust and cola your stomach would explode (immortalised in the Green Day song 'Poprocks & Coke'). Fortunately for us all, and especially those children who decided to test the rumour's accuracy by practical experimentation, this has since been debunked as nothing more than an urban myth. If you want that sort of reaction you will just have to resort to using Mentos!

WHY NOT TRY...

Wham Bar – chewy and fizzy

Flying Saucers – boldly going...

FLORAL GUMS

Length:
10 mm

Width:
10 mm

Depth:
6 mm

Weight:
0.6 g

Hero-2-Zero:
47 sec

Sometimes it can seem as if all pretences of logic have just flown out of the window. People like to eat oranges, so it is easy to understand why a confectioner would choose to create an orange-flavoured sweet. People enjoy the taste of lime and that of chocolate: ergo, the Chocolate Lime is a popular sweet shop choice. Now, I understand that many people enjoy flowers but, in the main, it is my perception that the derived pleasure is essentially visual. Why, then, would someone think that producing flower-flavoured sweets was a winning idea? Had they inadvertently stumbled across a fact that had remained undiscovered for millennia – the fact that the humble horticultural bloom tastes like the nectar of the gods? I can categorically state that no, they had not. That is, unless you have always imagined the heavenly delights of ambrosia to taste like the soap your grandmother uses.

I accept that many people thoroughly enjoy Floral Gums – they remain, after all, a best-seller in many sweet shops – but I cannot for one moment fathom why this should be. Equally curious is the fact that these loyal devotees of the Floral Gum insist on their supplies being of a single brand – those produced by Squirrel.

You would think that one speciality confection such as this would be enough to satisfy the florally inclined, but no! Produced by the same manufacturer are Cherry Lips – tiny bright red, crescent-shaped gums that taste nothing like the succulent fleshy fruit from which they take their name. Instead they're just like a different brand of soap. Fans of Floral Gums should give them a try.

FACT

Floral Gums were popular with children in wartime Britain because you got lots for your ration allowance.

WHY NOT TRY...

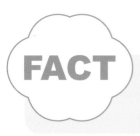

Parma Violets – because you obviously like flowers

Midget Gems – the small and fruity alternative

FLYING SAUCER

Length:
40 mm

Width:
40 mm

Depth:
15 mm

Weight:
1 g

Hero-2-Zero:
39 sec

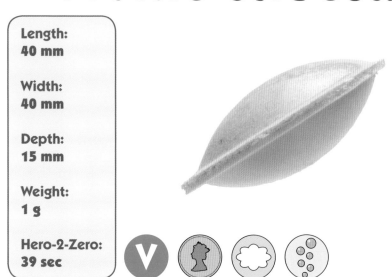

This is it! The big seller! In most sweet shops sales of flying saucers outstrip other confections by a considerable margin. Why? Well, not only are they truly delicious, but 100 grams is almost a jarful. There is little substitute for volume when sweets are involved.

The Flying Saucer consists of two convex, rigid discs of rather tasteless but brightly coloured corn-starch (a little like a turbocharged communion wafer) filled with delightfully fizzy and slightly citric sherbet. Placed whole in the mouth its lenticular shape allows it to be gently pressed against the roof of the mouth with the tongue where it instantly absorbs every last drop of saliva, leaving the taster feeling slightly parched and in need of refreshment. This is where the cleverly thought out science of the Flying Saucer comes into its own. Now saturated with oral fluids, the once hard shell loses shape and dissolves to release its taste-bud-tingling payload.

Surely one of the most satisfying experiences for any fan of sweets and candy!

One word of caution – always insist on fresh Flying Saucers as those left open to the atmosphere soon lose their outer crispness and the content will solidify.

FACT

The term 'Flying Saucer', used to refer to a UFO, was coined in 1947 after a sighting by Kenneth Arnold near Mount Rainer, Washington.

WHY NOT TRY...

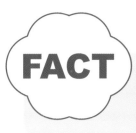

Fizz Wiz – tingly on the tongue

Sherbet Fountain – the classic sherbet confection

FRIED EGG

Length:
160 mm

Width:
20 mm

Depth:
20 mm

Weight:
14 g

Hero-2-Zero:
**18 sec
(chewed)
2 min 11 sec
(sucked)**

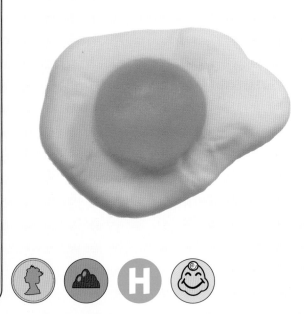

Like the Creme Egg, the Fried Egg is one of those confections that falls into the 'How do you eat yours?' category. Although it is clearly a single sweet, it is, like its albumen packed natural cousin, comprised of two distinct parts – a sweet and light foam 'white' and a deep yellow gummy 'yolk'.

The less confectionally aware amongst us might be tempted to consume the whole thing in one with nothing more than haphazard chomping, but what would be the point of that? The more astute will recognise that when a sweet is manufactured with two clear components such as these then a more considered approach should be taken. Separating the two halves, either with a pre-emptive nibble or whilst fully placed in the mouth, is an obvious answer and one which will allow the delights of the gummy yolk to be enjoyed rather than being lost to the dominant sweetness of the foam base.

Perhaps the perfect complementary sweet to the Fried Egg is the Gummi Bear. Whilst there is no obvious correlation between the two confections, the two go together like strawberries and champagne, highlighting each other's flavours to perfection.

FACT

The Fried Egg may have started it all many years ago but there is now a plethora of food-shaped foam sweets available from build-it-burgers to pizza slices. We are, however, yet to see a gummy potato.

WHY NOT TRY...

Gummi Bears – the modern classic

Cola Bottles – an essential penny accompaniment

FRUIT SALAD

Length:
25 mm

Width:
17 mm

Depth:
6 mm

Weight:
3 g

Hero-2-Zero:
1 min 16 sec

Another of the penny sweet essentials, the Fruit Salad has a sweet and juicy appeal that is far wider reaching than its aniseed counterpart, the Black Jack. Hidden in a brightly coloured wax wrapper, its luscious red and orange combination of raspberry and pineapple proves to be surprisingly thirst quenching and a truly unique flavour in the confectionery universe.

It appears, however, that the classic penny Fruit Salad has become smaller over the years – not by an enormous amount, but enough to be noticeable. As an alternative, a larger Fruit Salad Bar (about the size of a classic Wham Bar) is now available. But whilst it may duplicate the flavour of the original penny sweet, it could never match its charm.

The Barratt Fruit Salad is not to be confused with the product of the same name produced by Lions. This, a brightly coloured selection of juicy fruit gums, is an altogether different confection which, although worthy of commendation in its own right, pales into insignificance against the chewy original.

FACT

In the United States, chews like Fruit Salads are known as taffy.

WHY NOT TRY...

Black Jacks – because you can't have one without the other

Drumstick – fruity and chewy – what's not to like?

GOBSTOPPER

Standard

Diameter:
20 mm

Weight:
8 g

Hero-2-Zero:
56 min

Giant

Diameter:
40 mm

Weight:
56 g

Hero-2-Zero:
180 min

'You can suck 'em and suck 'em and suck 'em, and they'll never get any smaller.' So said Willy Wonka in Roald Dahl's *Charlie and the Chocolate Factory*. What was he talking about? The Everlasting Gobstopper, of course!

The Gobstopper is nothing less than a tuck-shop legend, and quite unlike any other confection available. Without exception, every other sweet in the shop can be eaten in more than one way. Some you can suck or chew, others you could suck or crunch. With the Gobstopper all you can do is suck – and keep sucking! For this is a confection not to be treated lightly.

Whatever its ultimate size, every Gobstopper starts its life as a single grain of sugar. Made using a method known as cold panning, liquid sugar is gradually added to a rotating pan. This covers each grain in a thin film which solidifies to form a hard shell. Incredibly, this process must be repeated more than 100 times over a two week period just to make one standard-sized Gobstopper (20 mm in diameter), although many can be made simultaneously in a single pan.

Even in its smallest form it is near impossible to consume a Gobstopper in a single sitting, and for this reason it is deemed perfectly acceptable to occasionally remove the confection from one's mouth to rest the jaw muscles.

For those looking for something a little more substantial, larger Gobstoppers are available. These include: the 40 mm Giant, which is of similar size to a golf ball; the 60 mm Monster, which would not look out of place on a snooker table; and the astonishing World's Biggest, which, at a tennis ball sized 70 mm, requires nothing less than a flip-top head to consume.

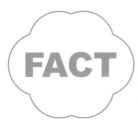

FACT In the United States, they are known as Jawbreakers.

WHY NOT TRY...

Aniseed Balls – like a mini gobstopper

Traffic Light Lolly – mouth filling and juicy

GOLD NUGGETS

Length:
13 mm
(average)

Width:
8 mm
(average)

Depth:
6 mm
(average)

Weight:
1 g
(average)

Hero-2-Zero:
40 sec

Popping the contents of a bag of Gold Nuggets in your mouth will instantly transport you back in time. Packed to overflowing with tiny, hard pieces of bright yellow gum, the little hessian sack complete with cartoon prospector is pure 1970s in every respect and would look perfectly in place on a shelf with a Corgi *Starsky & Hutch* Ford Torino and a game of Buckaroo.

Known also as Gold Rush, Gold Mine and Gold Rocks, its fruity flavour brings back memories of long hot summers, Raleigh Choppers and power cuts. But when you were eight years old, as yummy as this gum was, its flavour was the last thing on your mind. Gold Nuggets were all about the sack. Everything else in the sweet shop, if it was not sold naked, was wrapped in paper, cardboard, foil or plastic, none of which served any useful function once the confection had been consumed. The Gold Nugget sack was perfect for carrying everything: marbles, toy soldiers, pre-decimal currency – the potential was limited only by your imagination and the contents of your pockets. But why should this unparalleled usefulness be limited to your youth? Buy some Gold Nuggets now, relish the trip back in time and then use the bag to prevent your small change making a hole in the pockets of your best work trousers! Sometimes the best ideas are the old ones.

FACT To remove chewing gum from clothing squirt on some washing up liquid, add some salt and then rub off with another cloth.

WHY NOT TRY...

Anglo Bubbly – if you like your bubbles to be British

Cola Bottles – an essential penny accompaniment

GRAYS TEACAKES

Length:
30 mm

Width:
30 mm

Depth:
7 mm

Weight:
5 g

Hero-2-Zero:
4 min 38 sec

In addition to its revered Herbal, since the mid 1950s Grays of Dudley have been renowned for their Teacake. Often copied but never equalled, it takes the form of a sugar-coated medallion that is, appropriately, the colour of a strong cup of English Breakfast. The beauty, however, is that these ochre discs are gorgeously rough and uneven, with a truly home-crafted appearance that gives the impression that their hot, sticky mixture had been dropped from on high before being allowed to set.

Despite its warm sugary taste, when first placed in the mouth a Grays Teacake may seem a little hard – perhaps even uninviting. But let it warm for a moment and it will soon soften, releasing its superb combination of rich toffee, cinnamon and coconut. Incredibly moreish, it is all too easy to consume a hearty portion in one sitting.

Whilst sharing a common ingredient (coconut), the Grays Teacake should not under any circumstances be mistaken for the Toasted Teacake – an altogether different confection bearing no similarity in taste, texture or appearance.

FACT Some people call these Marzipan Teacakes despite there being no marzipan in sight.

WHY NOT TRY...

Toasted Teacakes – more delicious coconut

Coconut Mushrooms – light and fluffy with a unique shape

GUMMI BEAR

Length:
20 mm

Width:
12 mm

Depth:
10 mm

Weight:
2 g

Hero-2-Zero:
**11 sec
(chewed)
1 min 21 sec
(sucked)**

The world can thank German confectioner Hans Riegal of Bonn for the invention of the Gummi Bear or *Gummibär*. **HA**ns, **RI**egal, **BO**nn – is that starting to sound a little familiar? Riegal was, of course, the founder of Haribo, whose legacy has become one of the largest confectionery manufacturers in the world.

Inspired by both the humble little teddy bear and the somewhat larger and more real dancing bears widely seen across Germany at fairs, he created the two-for-a-pfennig Haribo Tanzbären – a bear-shaped fruit gum that, whilst bearing a striking similarity to the Gummi Bear we know today, was larger and slimmer. This became the company's most popular line until it was finally replaced in the mid 1960s when the modern-day Goldbears were introduced.

These little *Ursidae* are spectacularly tasty and possess that wonderful consistency that requires an initial hard bite to pierce the outer skin before your teeth sink effortlessly through the fruity flesh within. It can, however, come as a surprise to find that the Gummi Bear does not wholly follow the normal flavour/colour conventions of other sweets. True to form, the orange coloured bear is orange flavoured, the yellow tastes of lemon and the red of raspberry, and even the fact that the white bear is pineapple flavoured may not raise an eyebrow. Few, however, are aware that the green Gummi Bear is strawberry flavoured – a thoroughly useful fact to know when sharing a bag with friends!

FACT In 1925 Hans Riegel created the Schwarzer Bär – a little black bear made of liquorice.

WHY NOT TRY...

Fried Eggs – another gummy favourite

Fizzy Cola Bottles – jelly with a kick

HIGHLAND TOFFEE BAR

Length:
145 mm

Width:
25 mm

Depth:
5 mm

Weight:
19 g

Hero-2-Zero:
5 min 17 sec

Now, this is real Scottish comfort food! The Highland Toffee Bar, in one form or another, has graced the shelves of sweet emporiums north of the border for well over eighty years. In its original form it was known best as the Penny Dainty – a rock hard oblong toffee about an inch and a half in length, wrapped in a traditional and distinctive Black Watch tartan highlighted with green, white and red. Any wee bairn preparing to sample its delights would first grasp the Dainty in the palm of their hand, bounce it hard off the pavement to break it in two before placing both halves simultaneously into the mouth. Only then would the toffee be in a manageable state to consume without causing injury to the jaw.

The last of the Penny Dainties left the McCowan's Broxburn factory in 1969 (that's not strictly true as the management still possess one or two examples which look as good as the day they were manufactured) when its place in the corner shop was overtaken by the Highland Toffee Bar we know today. A good six inches in length, it is made of beautifully soft and creamy toffee that can be nibbled, sucked or chewed without causing any unwanted trips to the dentist.

FACT Andrew McCowan worked as a cattle herder and lemonade delivery boy before he set up his own confectionery company in Stenhousemuir in 1924.

WHY NOT TRY...

Bonbons – bite-sized morsels of dreamy, creamy toffee

Wham Bar – another creation from Millar McCowan

ICY CUP

Length: 10 mm	
Width: 10 mm	
Depth: 25 mm	
Weight: 4 g	
Hero-2-Zero: 44 sec	

If you are the kind of person who likes to eat Nutella straight from the jar, then the Icy Cup is the perfect confection for you. Combining silky smooth milk chocolate with blissful hazelnut it has a surprisingly cooling sensation in the mouth, almost minty in its freshness, and melts away effortlessly from the moment it makes contact with your tongue.

Produced by Scottish confectioners Hannah's of Johnstone, the Icy Cup has a truly unique retro appearance with each chocolate served in a miniature foil cupcake case red, gold, green, blue or purple in colour. This seemingly extravagant packaging adds beautifully to the feeling of indulgence: just extracting an Icy Cup from its foil case prior to consumption seems like a treat. This, in itself, is a task that must be performed carefully. First, the pleated sides must be gently stretched open before firmly pressing on the base of the foil to ease the confection free. Chocolatey heaven!

FACT

Icy Cups contain hazelnut paste and milk. Seventy-five per cent of the world's production of hazelnuts takes place in Ordu Province, Turkey – that's 625,000 tonnes, or about half a billion nuts every year!

WHY NOT TRY...

Cinder Toffee – sticky and sweet

Sweet Peanuts – more nutty delights

JAZZIES

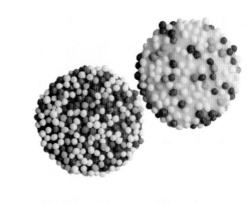

Length:
28 mm

Width:
28 mm

Depth:
4 mm

Weight:
2 g

Hero-2-Zero:
29 sec

Everyone knows that the chocolate button is yummy. One might be tempted to think that there would be no possible way to improve on its near perfect design. Smooth, silky, compact and discreet (there is no better confection for covert munching than a bag of Buttons) the chocolate button seemingly has it made. But then along came the Jazzie. What a fantastic idea! Take the perfection that is the chocolate drop and coat it in lots of lovely hundreds and thousands. The result – a multicoloured gem of a sweet that retains all the smoothness of the original but adds in a satisfying crunch.

There are, of course, numerous ways to eat this multicoloured delicacy. The most obvious is the simple munch; a clear alternative is the long, soothing suck. But for those for whom every sweet is an opportunity to play, the challenge must surely be to remove every single coloured adornment with the tongue before consuming the chocolate drop base as nature intended. Whoever said playing with your food was a bad thing has obviously never indulged in the delights of the Jazzie.

FACT Jazzies are also known as Disco Discs, Brown Gems or, in the case of the white chocolate variety, Snowies.

WHY NOT TRY...

White Mice – because white chocolate is the best

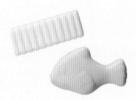

Fish & Chips – and these are the best of the best

JELLY BABIES

Length:
30 mm

Width:
18 mm

Depth:
15 mm

Weight:
6 g

Hero-2-Zero:
**32 sec
(chewed)
4 min 1 sec
(sucked)**

It is a common misapprehension that the humble Jelly Baby was born in 1919 but it was, in fact, conceived far earlier – in 1864, to be precise, by an Austrian confectioner by the name of Steinboch working for the now long defunct Lancastrian sweet manufacturer, Fryers. At this time, rather than being known as Jelly Babies, they were known by the rather more Dickensian and somewhat unfortunate title of Unclaimed Babies.

In 1919, following the end of World War One, Bassett re-launched the sugary infants as Peace Babies, a name which was kept until production was suspended, ironically, due to lack of raw materials due to the hostilities of World War Two. It wasn't until 1953 that the little sweets made their reappearance and were, at last, called Jelly Babies. Ever popular, the Bassett's Jelly Babies lost their generic appearance in the early 1990s when each coloured morsel took on its own name, shape and character. Is your favourite the lime-flavoured crying green Boofuls or the smiling strawberry red Brilliant?

For those more advanced in years there is always the wonderful alternative from Barnack Confectionery – the Jellyatric. This octogenarian assortment includes lemon-flavoured Bill Bird the pigeon fancier, lime-flavoured Olive Green with her knitting, orange Frau Zimmer with her Zimmer frame and raspberry-flavoured Bryan Bashful, the retired professor.

 **FACT** Bassett's make more than a billion Jelly Babies every year!

WHY NOT TRY...

 **Wine Gums – steeped in tradition**

 **Jelly Beans – the perfect pocket treat**

JELLY BEAN

Length:
24 mm

Width:
10 mm

Depth:
10 mm

Weight:
2 g

Hero-2-Zero:
**27 sec
(chewed)
1 min 50 sec
(sucked)**

Jelly Beans essentially fall into one of two different camps. There are what you might call the standard, or regular, Jelly Beans – these are brightly coloured, very sweet, have a fruity shell, are about the size of a cashew nut and are sold en masse in sweet shops from jars. They cost no more than any other sweets.

Then you have what are called Gourmet Jelly Beans. Sold in countless flavours they are often combined in the mouth to make Jelly Bean cocktails using recipes gleaned from enthusiastic websites. They are fun, they are wacky, they are trendy and they are expensive. Think of regular Jelly Beans as Microsoft and Gourmet Jelly Beans as Apple. Now you've got it!

The gourmet's Gourmet Jelly Bean is, of course, the Jelly Belly. First introduced in the middle of the 1970s and now sold in 50 different varieties, the Jelly Belly, unlike others brands, is flavoured all the way through. Each bean is truly crafted and takes anything from one to three weeks to manufacture. Despite this time-consuming process, two million beans roll off the Jelly Belly production line every single hour – that's 14 billion beans per year!

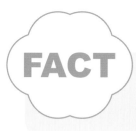

FACT

Take a Toasted Marshmallow, a Caramel Apple and a Lemon Lime Jelly Belly to make a Sucker's Guide Special!

WHY NOT TRY...

Gummi Bears – small and perfectly formed

Liquorice Comfits and Torpedoes – the liquorice alternative

JESMONA
BLACK BULLETS

Diameter:
19 mm

Weight:
6 g

Hero-2-Zero:
5 min 57 sec

You may not realise this, but you love Jesmona Black Bullets. These very traditional peppermint-flavoured boiled sweets are one of the great hidden treasures of the confectionery world.

Quite when the Black Bullet was first invented nobody can be sure, but the Jesmona name, derived from the Jesmond area of Newcastle-upon-Tyne, has been with us since 1906. Ever popular with the hard-working miners, shipbuilders and steelworkers who were not permitted to smoke at work (and you thought that was a new idea!) its cool, clean taste was a breath of fresh air in this grimy industrial heartland.

Calling a sweet a bullet was not at all uncommon in the North East of England but, like the sweet itself, the origins of the term are surrounded in a certain level of mystery. One theory is that the sweets were originally made using the moulds for musket balls. This may or may not be true – it's certainly not how they are made today – but there is no denying the fact that the Black Bullet's satisfying shape sits perfectly on the tongue.

Whilst available loose from the jar in individual cellophane wrappers, there is nothing quite like buying a tin in which they are supplied naked and ready to devour. If nothing else, the wonderful black and white canister makes a spectacular desk accessory for the true confectionery fanatic.

FACT

Whilst traditional in appearance, Jesmona Black Bullets were ahead of their time in being made entirely of natural ingredients.

WHY NOT TRY...

Uncle Joe's Mint Balls – another warming classic

Bull's Eyes – straight out of *Just William*

LIQUORICE ALLSORTS

Length:
15–25 mm

Width:
10–20 mm

Depth:
8–15 mm

Weight:
4–7 mm

Hero-2-Zero:
31 sec
(average)

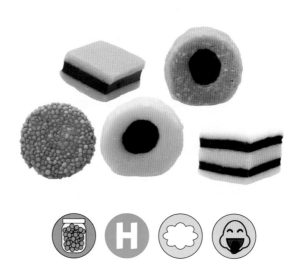

If it wasn't for the clumsy nature of Bassett's salesman Charlie Thompson, we would not have the edible playground that is the Liquorice Allsort. He had taken a selection of new liquorices and cream paste sweets to show to a client but, despite his pressing sales technique, none were purchased. Rather put out by the poor response to his efforts, Thompson busily gathered together his sample boxes and trays, only to spill the contents all over the table and floor. He quickly began to scoop the errant confections together but was stopped in his tracks as the wholesaler proclaimed that this mixture was what he was after! The Liquorice Allsort was born.

The great thing about Liquorice Allsorts is that there are so many varieties and so many ways of eating them. The layered ones are just begging to be dissected into component parts, the pink and yellow round coconut ones are dying to be nibbled and the paste-filled tubular ones must be rolled out flat. Curiously, one of the most popular Liquorice Allsorts is completely liquorice free – the Spog. These little pink and blue aniseed jellies may be put in the mouth whole, but must be stripped totally clean of their bobbles before any chewing takes place. There are so many different eating combinations that it would, in fact, be possible to munch your way through an entire bag of Allsorts without once having to repeat yourself.

FACT Bertie Bassett was born on 1 January 1929, making him 16 days older than Popeye.

WHY NOT TRY...

Catherine Wheels – 'cos it's got a Spog in the middle!

Pontefract Cakes – liquorice in the purest form

LIQUORICE PIPE

Length:
110 mm

Width:
10 mm

Depth:
10 mm

Weight:
17 g

Hero-2-Zero:
cannot be
rushed

The world is packed full of regulations and laws, mostly unwritten, describing what passes as permissible behaviour when in possession of confectionery items – before consuming a Jelly Baby you must first bite off its head (or its legs if you are my sister), Fried Eggs must first have their gummy yolks removed, and so on. The Liquorice Pipe is no different. After placing its inky black bowl in your hand for the first time, admiring the bright red bobbles (known as nonpareils if you're in the trade) and raising it towards your mouth, you must first make a semi-convincing Popeye impression ('Ahh ak ak ak ak ak!') before indulging further in its pleasures.

With this ritual safely out of the way you may now enjoy the Pipe's rich liquorice flavour. Holding it clamped between your teeth for a while is more than acceptable, although you must be prepared for the obligatory liquorice stain on your lip that accompanies this practice. Having steadily worked your way past the mouthpiece and stem you will finally be left with the substantial lump of liquorice that makes up the bowl. This is the prize for your hard work and should, excessive as it may seem, be consumed in one.

Now, where can I buy myself a liquorice smoking jacket and a pair of liquorice slippers?

FACT

Incredibly, stores used to sell Junior Smokers Kits featuring Liquorice Pipes, Liquorice Tobacco and Candy Cigarettes as Christmas gifts!

WHY NOT TRY...

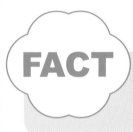

Chocolate Cigarettes – and you can still sit inside

Spanish Gold – 'cos you need something to stuff in your pipe

LOVE HEARTS

Length:	20 mm
Width:	20 mm
Depth:	5 mm
Weight:	1 g
Hero-2-Zero:	1 min 32 sec (sucked)

Every child gets to an age when the opposite sex ceases to be an irritation and instead becomes an obsession. How then, when wooing the girl or boy of their dreams, does an eleven-year-old profess their undying love? If you're a boy then giving flowers is a big no-no. For a start it is far too showy and anyway, it would result in instant ridicule from your peers. If you're a girl the graffiti on your exercise book seemed a great idea at the time but now you've got to hand it in to Mrs Johnson for marking and you know what she thinks about things like that.

The solution is the Love Heart – a fizzy little sweet reminiscent of Fizzers and Refreshers embossed with the perfect message to convey your own heart's desire. That used to mean something like 'Dream Girl', 'Be Mine', 'It's Love' or 'Only You' but these days things seem to have changed a little with messages like 'Txt Me', 'Email Me' and the somewhat curious 'Fax Me' (do many teenagers possess fax machines – and is it really that romantic a sentiment to sit there watching a love… brrr… letter… brrr… trickle… brrr… out?).

You can, of course, go one stage further in keeping up with the trends of today. Slightly less romantic but still made by Swizzels Matlow are Whatevers. Sold exclusively by a supermarket chain, they abandon the sweet nothings of their tender cousins and instead state 'As If', 'Bothered', 'In It' and the delightful 'Chav'.

Oh, how times have changed!

FACT

Since the first Love Hearts sweets were made in 1950 there have been well over 100 different messages, the most popular of which is, quite simply, 'I Love You'.

WHY NOT TRY...

Candy Letters – write sweet messages

Swizzels Double Lolly – two lip-smacking flavours on one stick

MIDGET GEMS

Length:	
8 mm	

Width:
8 mm

Depth:
11 mm

Weight:
2 g

Hero-2-Zero:
41 sec

There are storm clouds gathering over the Yorkshire mill-town of Cleckheaton, for it is here that dark forces are at work threatening to change forever a tradition that has stood firm for over a century.

In 1903, when Albert and Frank Hardhill established their company in a row of converted cottages on Westgate they had a vision – to bring a delicious, multicoloured selection of sweets to the good people of the north. A gem of a sweet – the Midget Gem – five different fruity flavoured treats in orange, green, red, yellow, white and, most importantly, a black one tasting of liquorice. They succeeded, and Lion Confectionery was born.

For decades the joys of the Midget Gem were almost the exclusive preserve of those living in the north of the country. They had, of course, found their way elsewhere, but few people in these far-off climes really knew of their sublime pleasures. Then, in 2005, the opportunity arose for this regional delicacy to go global as Lion was brought into the Cadbury Trebor Bassett family.

At first this seemed like a sweet marriage made in heaven. Surely the more Midget Gems the better? But fame comes at a price and the victim in this tragedy is set to be the black Gem. Apparently, in this day and age, the prospect of finding a liquorice sweet amongst fruity neighbours would be too much of a shock for the uninitiated, so it must change. Its replacement is set to be an all too predictable blackcurrant. However, keeping an emergency quantity of Poor Bens to hand offers a simple solution to this purchasing predicament. As a further act of defiance I would recommend that you post the offending charlatan confections back to Lion stating your dissatisfaction.

Even in the sweet world of confectionery, life can be so unfair!

FACT

Such was the uproar when Maynards announced the demise of the traditional black Midget Gem an online petition was organised to try and reverse their decision.

WHY NOT TRY...

Floral Gums – now with added chrysanthemums

Liquorice Gums – because you love the black ones

MILK BOTTLE

Length:
28 mm

Width:
15 mm

Depth:
18 mm

Weight:
3 g

Hero-2-Zero:
**20 sec
(chewed)
2 min 47 sec
(sucked)**

If you glued a prancing horse on the front of an Austin Maxi it would not make it a Ferrari. Similarly, if you produce a creamy white sweet in the shape of a bottle it does not make it a Milk Bottle. Would somebody please tell that to the countless confectionery manufacturers who insist on selling us sweets that are pale comparisons of the originals we know and love so well? There are a number of different sweets on the market that claim to be Milk Bottles, but few of these can match for taste, texture and sheer enjoyment the original that we all remember from our youth. It was not rubbery. It did not shine. It did not taste of pineapple. (Yes, there is a pineapple flavoured so-called Milk Bottle out there!)

The classic Milk Bottle Gum should arrive dusted in a liberal coating of starch (left over from the manufacturing process where it ensures the bottles don't become glued to the mould), be hard when first placed in the mouth and then become smooth and slightly sticky. Above all, it should be shaped like a proper milk bottle (not some continental interpretation of one) and should actually contain milk.

Mention should also be made of Smiths Milk Chews, an altogether different milky confection sold in a stick pack that stands up in its own right as a true sweet shop classic and is not unlike a milky Fruitella. Although hard to come by, these are well worth experimenting with. They may not be a true Milk Bottle Gum but they are a worthy alternative.

FACT

Milk Bottle Gums contain real milk but you'd need to eat almost 1,200 of them to consume a pint of the white stuff.

WHY NOT TRY...

Fried Eggs – if gums get you going

Cola Bottles – for the bottle fanatic

MINT HUMBUG

Length:
26 mm

Width:
26 mm

Depth:
16 mm

Weight:
11 g

Hero-2-Zero:
6 min 32 sec

'"Bah," said Scrooge, "Humbug!"' It would be wonderful to inform you that the humble Mint Humbug has its origins in the works of Charles Dickens but, alas, no – Ebenezer Scrooge was merely using an age-old term for gibberish. However, all is not lost. The *Oxford Dictionary of English* tells us that as early as 1825, almost twenty years before Dickens penned *A Christmas Carol*, the word 'humbug' was in use in reference to a type of sweet.

As Dickens novels are rightly considered classics of literature, so the Mint Humbug is hailed as a classic of the confectioner's shelf. There are several versions of the sweet currently available, all of which can claim their own individual merits. Some are a traditional lozenge shape, others are circular, whilst many of the premium and home-made varieties are twisted. All, however, share a delicious brown and white striped hard peppermint shell and a gorgeously sticky soft centre.

Incredibly, the sweets are made by first creating a giant striped Humbug about the size of a bed pillow and gradually stretching and rolling it until it becomes rope-like and small enough to cut into individual sweets. Even in this age of technology and automation much of this process is completed by hand. Sometimes the old methods are the best!

FACT

In 2001, a 75 cm long, 30 kg Mint Humbug believed to be the world's largest was stolen from the offices of a TV station by thieves and never recovered.

WHY NOT TRY...

Bull's Eyes – eminently suckable

Uncle Joe's Mint Balls – as original as mints get

MOJO

Length:
31 mm

Width:
19 mm

Depth:
9 mm

Weight:
6 g

Hero-2-Zero:
1 min 37 sec

Long before Austin Powers brought his own particular slant to the word 'mojo', we had the Mojo chew and, as the sweets themselves proclaim, 'Respect the Mojo!' For decades the world of the penny chew had been dominated by just two offerings – the Black Jack and the Fruit Salad. Other chews, such as Opal Fruits and Fruitella, were available but these were sold in packets, and to an eight-year-old this method of purchase is seen as nothing less than a restriction of trade and the antithesis of why the penny sweet selection was created in the first place. Then came the Mojo, and with it a revolution in tuck shop spending habits.

This all-new chew was softer, tastier and slightly larger than its old school opposition and, more importantly, was offered in a choice of flavours – banana, cola, orange, raspberry and, critically in this day and age, spearmint. Why the importance of spearmint, you may ask? Remember Pacers – the minty version of the Opal Fruit with the green and white stripes that used to act as a welcome interlude on summer holiday car journeys but sadly fell by the confectionery wayside? The spearmint Mojo has exactly the same taste and texture! Its heritage may be different, but the end result is identical. Oh, bliss!

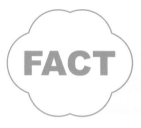

FACT

All Mojos, apart from the cola ones, are halal approved.

WHY NOT TRY...

Drumstick – the big chew on a stick

Fruit Salad – the fruity original

NERDS

Length:
6 mm
(average)

Width:
4 mm
(average)

Depth:
5 mm
(average)

Weight:
3 g
(average)

Hero-2-Zero:
14 sec

Sometimes those Americans get to have all of the fun. Whilst on this side of the Atlantic we had to put up with the somewhat uninspired and unimaginative tic-tac – those little rock-hard white, green and orange tablets that looked more like something that would be prescribed by your local GP – in the early 1980s, our stateside cousins were treated to an alternative that was infinitely more fun-packed and exciting – the Nerd.

More colourful than a Brazilian bartender's shirt, Nerds are bright, shiny and lots of fun. If the regular shaped tic-tacs in their clear, hard plastic box with the flip-lid are the accountants of the confectionery world, then Nerds are the surfing instructors. Even the flavours are fun – tic-tacs have their peppermint and their orange and lime, but Nerds have Watermelon and Wild Cherry, or Amped Apple and Lightning Lemon Sour.

Thankfully for us all, somebody had the bright idea of taking the Nerds on a European vacation, and in the late 1980s they hit the shores of the United Kingdom. Typical of the Americans – late again! Unsurprisingly, they were an instant hit, although this may have been due to the fact that each time a new flavour was released it came packaged inside a Nerd figurine. Remember – free booty is everything in the sweet world.

Unfortunately, Nerds are once again hard to come by in the United Kingdom but fear not: they can be hunted down through specialist retailers.

FACT

Nerds also used to be available as a breakfast cereal which came in a divided box with two flavours, just like the sweets.

Millions – small enough to munch in secret

Poppets – the classic pop-in-the-mouth treat

PARMA VIOLETS

Length:
12 mm

Width:
12 mm

Depth:
4 mm

Weight:
7 g

Hero-2-Zero:
31 sec

Parma Violets are evil. There, I've said it – and nothing short of divine intervention from a host of heavenly angels dressed in lilac gowns would have me believe otherwise.

Incredibly, this is not another weird creation from the folk who brought you Floral Gums and Cherry Lips, but a product from those masters of the tuck shop treat, Swizzels Matlow. How on earth could the genius that brought us the Fizzer, the Drumstick and the hallowed Double Dip create such an abomination? This is what McCartney's Frog Chorus was to The Beatles' *The White Album*.

I so dearly wish I could find some solitary redeeming feature that would offer a ray of salvation and hope for the Parma Violet but, alas, it does not exist. The only solution, should you be so unfortunate to come into possession of a pack, is to set them aside, wait for Halloween and then foist them onto some poor trick-or-treating five-year-old dressed as a pumpkin. It is, after all, the appropriate time of year for frightening small children.

Having said all that, whether you love them or hate them, Parma Violets rightfully deserve their place in this book as a classic confection – let's hope they continue to cause controversy for years to come.

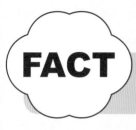

FACT In a survey of 7,500 people, Parma Violets topped the table of Sweets We Love to Hate.

WHY NOT TRY...

Floral Gums – another speciality confection

Love Hearts – the sweet alternative

PINK SHRIMP

Length:
30 mm

Width:
18 mm

Depth:
17 mm

Weight:
2 g

Hero-2-Zero:
25 sec

Whilst other classic champions of the corner shop penny-sweet selection translate well to adult life, the Cola Bottle and the Fruit Salad for example, the same cannot be said of the Pink Shrimp. The reason why? The Pink Shrimp is possibly the sweetest substance known to man. If you have never before tasted one, nothing can quite prepare you fully for the saccharine onslaught that accompanies the experience. This is not to say that the Pink Shrimp is unpleasant in any way – merely that it is a taste best suited to those who have not yet reached double figures in the age stakes.

Then there is the shape. A decapod crustacean is not the most obvious choice for a winning penny confection, especially when you consider the fact that it also bears more than a passing resemblance to a human ear – thoughts of eight-year-olds re-enacting scenes from *Reservoir Dogs* spring to mind. The eating experience is quite straightforward – crumbling easily in the mouth with a vaguely fruity but ultimately indiscernible flavour – but all of the time the unavoidable aspartame overtones dominate.

WHY NOT TRY...

Anglo Bubbly – for longer-lasting flavour

Fish & Chips – white chocolate aquatics

PONTEFRACT CAKE

Length:
25 mm

Width:
25 mm

Depth:
5 mm

Weight:
4 g

Hero-2-Zero:
46 sec

When we think of liquorice we often imagine it to be a very British thing. Of course other countries have their liquorice – the Finns with their *salmiak*, a salty variety, the Australians with their newfangled natural products – but none seem to take it on as part of the very fabric of the nation in the same way as the Brits. Indeed, empires have been built on the stuff. It is, therefore, a curious fact that the key raw material – the liquorice root – is not indigenous to these shores but, in fact, a native of the Mediterranean and Asia.

Funny to imagine that in this day and age we might well not have the Liquorice Pipe, the Sherbet Fountain and, of course, the Pontefract Cake had it not been for the fifteenth-century intervention of a number of Dominican monks who imported *Glycyrrhiza glabra*, the plant from which the liquorice root is extracted, for its medicinal properties.

The Pomfret Cake was first introduced in 1614 when Sir George Saville of Lupsett lent his seal to a small liquorice-based cake produced in Pontefract

– a town in the centre of the English liquorice growing heartland. At first these small cakes were manufactured to provide relief from stomach aches and coughs but then, in 1760, an entrepreneurial apothecary named George Dunhill did a simple but amazing thing – he added sugar and the Pontefract Cake as we know and love it was born.

Beautifully soft and appetising, assuming as always that you're a fan of the black stuff, the Pontefract Cake is one of the true classics of British confectionery.

FACT Pontefract Cakes were originally embossed by hand. A skilled stamper would press over 20,000 cakes every day.

WHY NOT TRY...

 **Liquorice Pipe – for a little fun**

 **Liquorice Gums – the long-lasting alternative**

POPPETS

Length:
15 mm

Width:
15 mm

Depth:
3 mm

Weight:
2 g

Hero-2-Zero:
29 sec

For a long time I thought that the Paynes Poppet was a speciality sweet that was best at home tucked inside one of those tartan shopping trolleys alongside a fold up plastic rain hat and the local bus timetable. Quite frankly, I considered the Poppet to be the confection of little old ladies. Now, I should make it totally clear that this association is perfectly acceptable – after all, different sweets will appeal to different age groups. I'm not expecting your average octogenarian to show a particularly high level of interest in Fizz Wiz or Nerds and, conversely, I can't imagine many ten-year-olds heading into the nearest sweet shop and asking for a bag of Army & Navy.

A veteran of the confectionery counter, the Paynes Poppet has been with us since 1937. Supplied in a handy little box designed to prevent the entire contents decanting into your hand in one go (some might actually see this as a potential design flaw), these chocolate-covered morsels are available with a number of different centres – toffee, mint, raisin and orange being the current selection, although previous incarnations have included peanut and crunchy. In an attempt to shake off a less than trendy image, Poppets have a new and improved selection of flavours and are now sold in brightly coloured packaging adorned with retro images like the space hopper, the Rubik's cube and, curiously, a garden gnome. Whether they are likely to attain a must-have status akin to the mobile phone and iPod is another matter but, for once, the new version of a sweet appears to be an improvement on the old.

FACT Breakfast TV favourites Zig and Zag helped promote Poppets in the 1990s.

WHY NOT TRY...

Bonbons – if toffee is your choice

Nerds – another box of fun

RHUBARB & CUSTARD

Length:
30 mm

Width:
16 mm

Depth:
16 mm

Weight:
8 mm

Hero-2-Zero:
7 min 19 sec

Rhubarb & Custard! What a wonderful combination – especially when the two are complemented by a healthy layer of crumble. Alas, in candy form the crumble is absent; however, the remaining sweet and sour duet is one of the confectionery retailer's greatest treasures.

They are essentially sold in two forms. The first is a curious soft tubular chew manufactured in rather shocking shades of green, yellow and pink. Although sharp, fruity and not at all unpleasant, they do struggle to capture the delights of their natural namesake (well, custard is almost natural) and are perhaps best left alone. On the other hand (or in the other bag) is the alternative – a red and yellow, individually wrapped hard-boiled confection that offers the sucker all the acidity of real rhubarb whilst subtly combining the sweet creamy flavours of vanilla custard.

There is only one way to eat a real Rhubarb & Custard sweet and that is to suck, suck and suck some more. Doing so encourages you to curl your tongue around the lozenge and experience the contrasting taste sensations to their full capacity. A sweet of the highest order, indeed – part, in fact, of the unofficial confectionery royal family.

FACT

Until recently, 90 per cent of the world's rhubarb was grown in a tiny area of Yorkshire known as the Rhubarb Triangle.

WHY NOT TRY...

Chocolate Limes – sharp and chocolatey

Sherbet Lemons – just as sharp and with a fizzy edge

SHERBET DIP DAB

Length:
130 mm

Width:
100 mm

Depth:
15 mm

Weight:
26 g

Hero-2-Zero:
12 min 3 sec

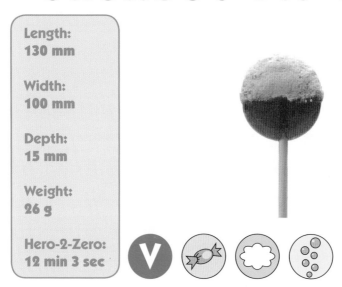

The Sherbet Dip Dab is the reason that school satchels have shoulder straps. After all, why else would you need both of your hands free on the walk home? Whilst it may not be considered a design classic like its close relative the Sherbet Fountain, the Dip Dab's fun and simplicity has won it many fans and a warm place in the hearts of countless sweet lovers. The explanation for this is, to my mind, all about tools.

People like tools. Why? Because tools not only have form but they have function. Just as ancient man used a flint axe to fashion arrow heads and twenty-first-century man uses a screwdriver to open uncooperative tins of paint and assemble flat-pack furniture from IKEA, so the indulger of a Sherbet Dip Dab can use the flat and very tasty strawberry lollipop to transfer sherbet from a little yellow bag to a big pink tongue.

Like any good tool, the Dip Dab is simple to use but takes time and practice to truly master – too much errant sucking and the sherbet will outlast the lolly. But, as they say, practice makes perfect, so what other motivation do you need?

FACT The Sherbet Dip Dab has survived but, alas, the same cannot be said for its citrus flavoured cousin the Lemonade Dipper – its familiar green and white wrapper has long since departed the sweet shop's shelves.

WHY NOT TRY...

Fizz Wiz – feed your brain

Sherbet Fountain – replace the swizzle stick with a liquorice stick

SHERBET FOUNTAIN

Length:
110 mm

Width:
25 mm

Depth:
25 mm

Weight:
34 g

Hero-2-Zero:
14 min 38 sec

The Sherbet Fountain is a wonderful example of genius – flawed genius. We all know how we are meant to consume a Sherbet Fountain – after all, we have been given an obvious enough clue by the way the hollow liquorice stick protrudes from the top of the yellow paper tube like a fuse from a stick of dynamite.

Yes, in a perfect world it would just take a quick bite from the top of the liquorice (if you're a young boy this would be done as if pulling the pin from a hand-grenade with your teeth) and then you could devour the effervescent content by simply sucking it through the newly created edible straw.

If only it worked like that! Biting the nib off the liquorice is not a problem, but try and suck the sherbet through it and a dry fizzing dust will consume your airway, invoking an uncontrollable coughing fit of epic proportion. In the delay caused by the commotion the moisture from your attempted inhalation will have caused the remaining sherbet in the liquorice tube to take on the consistency of drying cement, thus wholly preventing any further sucking action.

But here is the genius of the Sherbet Fountain because, far from having rendered the confection useless, the liquorice straw merely changes its role – becoming, instead, a perfect scoop to dip into the open packet and recover the remaining contents.

The Sherbet Fountain – almost perfect in a uniquely British way.

FACT

A Sherbet Fountain makes an appearance in the retro BBC TV series *Life on Mars* in the hands of DCI Gene Hunt.

WHY NOT TRY...

Sherbet Dip Dab – if you prefer to dip

Bassetti Liquorice Stick – the ideal sherbet dipping tool

SHERBET LEMON

Length:	
30 mm	

Width:
20 mm

Depth:
15 mm

Weight:
8 g

Hero-2-Zero:
6 min 51 sec

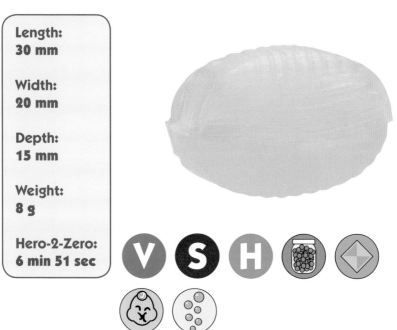

Sherbet Lemons – the thinking man's confection. Or thinking woman's, for that matter. Whatever the semantics, there is no doubting the fact that the Sherbet Lemon is the ideal accompaniment for any concerted bout of pondering. Wherever an empty bag of Sherbet Lemons lies, a great scholar once sat.

There is something curious about the sharp tasting hard outer shell that cleanses the soul and serves to concentrate the mind – its effervescent filling creating a welcome highlight and acting as a timely reminder that it will soon, once again, be time to delve into the paper bag to select another sweet. Ah yes, the paper bag – an essential component to the Sherbet Lemon experience. When eaten slowly, the last few sweets should become slightly sticky, causing them to bond to each other and to the bag. If timed to perfection, these rogue confections should pull away with a satisfying little tug but if left too long they are liable to pick up unwelcome scraps of paper which will interrupt the pleasure of the eating process. As with any confection, preparation is the key – to fail to prepare is to prepare to fail.

FACT In the Harry Potter series Professor Dumbledore's office password is 'Sherbet Lemons'.

WHY NOT TRY...

 **Chocolate Limes – if you prefer chocolate to fizz**

 **Rhubarb & Custard – sharp and creamy**

SOUR APPLE

Length: **15 mm**	
Width: **15 mm**	
Depth: **15 mm**	
Weight: **7 g**	
Hero-2-Zero: **6 min 20 sec**	

Today we are used to our Haribo Tangfastics, Sour Cherry Wham Bars and Brain Lickers. Even old favourites like Fruit Pastilles and Wine Gums are being offered in sour varieties. But once upon a time, confections were invariably sweet and, to most, the idea of sucking on something that tasted like a slice of raw lemon was a rather unattractive proposition.

Then along came the Sour Apple – the first sweet truly capable of making you pull facial expressions reminiscent of a bulldog chewing the proverbial wasp. Acidic and sharp to the extreme, it was a revelation, instantly winning friends and admirers from existing, candy addicts and converting others for whom regular confectionery had proved far too saccharine.

There are essentially two varieties available. The first is an all-green relative of the Kola Kube whose abrasive sugar coating matches well the tartness experienced in its consumption. The second and more common alternative is a spheroid – red and green in colour – dusted only in a fine layer of icing sugar. This version is, perhaps, gentler on the palate but no less enjoyable. Both, however, should be consumed with a certain level of care as too many can easily cause painful mouth ulcers. How we suffer for our art!

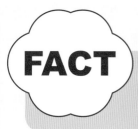

FACT The acid in sour sweets can do more damage to your tooth enamel than their sweet counterparts, so remember to brush well!

WHY NOT TRY...

Fizzy Cola Bottles – sour with a jelly base

Wham Bar – now there's a sour one!

SPANISH GOLD

Length:
25 mm
(average)

Width:
2 mm
(average)

Depth:
2 mm
(average)

Weight:
1 g
(average)

Hero-2-Zero:
37 sec
(per mouthful)

Once upon a time it was perfectly acceptable for a young boy to own a catapult, play with a cap gun and kick a tin can down the street. There were no claims of yobbish behaviour or cries for the instant instigation of an ASBO – it was all just seen as the exuberance of youth and part of the growing up process. In those happy days it was also possible to pop into the local corner shop and purchase a Liquorice Pipe and a pouch of Spanish Gold without someone claiming that it would only lead to the subsequent ruination of one's health.

Like Candy Cigarettes – sorry, Candy *Sticks* – Spanish Gold has undergone a facelift over the years. Also known as Sweet Tobacco, it was once sold in newsagents and corner shops next to the Fruit Salads and Black Jacks in little paper or plastic bags perfectly copying the pouches of real tobacco like Drum and Old Holborn packed into the shelves behind the counter under the guard of the watchful shopkeeper. After all, what better way for a youngster to live up to family expectations than to emulate with candy their father's spluttering forty-a-day Rothmans habit?

Now it is sold straight from the jar, there is no mention of its pseudo-smoking past in sight. A simple concoction of shredded desiccated coconut with a dusted brown sugar coating, it is a pleasure to eat, seems to last forever and, best of all, unlike its real tobacco counterparts you don't have to go outside to enjoy it.

FACT Original Spanish Gold pouches featured a picture of a galleon on the high seas.

WHY NOT TRY...

Chocolate Cigarettes – if you don't like to roll your own

Toasted Teacakes – sweet, sweet coconut

SWEET PEANUT

Length:
35 mm

Width:
18 mm

Depth:
18 mm

Weight:
8 g

Hero-2-Zero:
4 min 13 sec

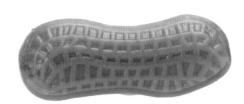

The Sweet Peanut offers yet another glorious time-warp to a bygone age and unlike so many other offerings it is actually a sweet that tastes how it looks. No cryptic concoctions here – just peanuts… and butterscotch!

Butterscotch is a wonderful thing. Invented in the early nineteenth century by Doncaster confectioner Samuel Parkinson, it has a unique velvety taste with hints of both toffee and caramel – a sublime combination if ever there was one. In the case of the Sweet Peanut it acts as a perfect housing for a crisp and crunchy peanut cracknel core.

The eating experience of the Sweet Peanut is quite unique in confectionery circles. Initial sucking leads one to think that it is yet another boiled sweet; however, before long the brittle nucleus starts to crumble away, turning the whole thing into a satisfyingly crunchable nutty delight. Once you get started you really can't help but chomp away and, as such, the Hero-2-Zero rating of the Sweet Peanut is surprisingly low for a hard confection. Pay heed to this and also to the fact that they are monumentally moreish – this combination tends to result in a bagful lasting a pitifully short time.

FACT Peanuts are not nuts! They are legumes, just like beans, peas and lentils.

WHY NOT TRY...

Barley Sugar – the age old favourite

Icy Cups – chocolate with a nutty twist

SWIZZELS
DOUBLE LOLLY

Length:
87 mm
(inc stick)

Width:
29 mm

Depth:
29 mm

Weight:
13 g

Hero-2-Zero:
7 min 52 sec

In certain circumstances Swizzels Double Lollies can give you headaches. Now, before the libel lawyers go reaching for their pens this is not because of some strange colouring or additive or, in fact, anything that those lovely people at Swizzels Matlow have done. With its heavy, rock-hard globe and slightly flexible plastic stick the Double Lolly's dubious reputation comes from the fact that, in the hands of a mischievous tyke in the tuck shop queue, it becomes a serious example of candy based combat hardware – a veritable confection of mass destruction – perfect for dispatching a well-placed crack over the skull of an unsuspecting classmate.

In eating, however, the Double Lolly is a friendlier affair. Effectively a huge Refresher on a stick (the proper hard fizzy ones, not the chewy imposter!) it proves to be both long lasting and flavoursome. Those with time on their hands can also indulge their artistic tendencies – the lolly's alabaster-like head being the perfect material for idle carving in between sucks.

For those seeking the ultimate Swizzels thrill there is the Mega Double Lolly which, weighing in at a hefty 32 grams (two and a half times the size of the standard edition), offers the scope for extended sucking, enlarged sculpting and increased cranial damage.

FACT

It's called a Double Lolly because there are two flavours on the top of every stick.

WHY NOT TRY...

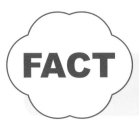

Candy Necklace – the ultimate accessory

Double Dip – try it with some sherbet

TOASTED TEACAKE

Length:
27 mm

Width:
27 mm

Depth:
13 mm

Weight:
6 g

Hero-2-Zero:
50 sec

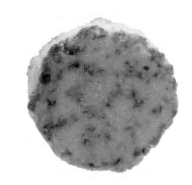

Not to be confused with the harder and flatter Grays Teacake, the Toasted Teacake is yet another favourite that has graced sweet-shop jars for many a decade. People often say that the best ideas are also the simplest and if ever proof were needed this confection would be the perfect example, for it is little more than shredded coconut bound with a little sugar and pressed hard into an inch-wide medallion. As a *pièce de résistance* the top and bottom are lightly toasted to an autumnal golden brown.

Melt-in-the-mouth is a term frequently overused when describing good food but there is no expression better suited to the sensation experienced when a Toasted Teacake is placed in the mouth. The preferred method of consumption is to first prime the mouth with a little saliva before sucking on the confection, allowing the binding sugar to melt away. This will leave you with a mouthful of moist, sweet coconut that can be satisfyingly chewed to release yet more flavour.

FACT Alongside marshmallows, Toasted Teacakes make an excellent accompaniment to a chocolate fondue.

WHY NOT TRY...

Coconut Mushrooms – great for nibbling

Grays Teacakes – longer lasting coconut pleasure

WHAM BAR

Length:
145 mm

Width:
25 mm

Depth:
5 mm

Weight:
22 g

Hero-2-Zero:
6 min 11 sec

Sinclair Spectrums, The Human League, Maggie Thatcher, Sun-in hair highlights, mobile phones the size of house bricks – all indisputable icons of the 1980s. But any defining list of the 1980s is surely incomplete if it doesn't include the Wham Bar – that oversized chew that is both fruity and fizzy and was an essential tuck shop purchase at least once a week.

Produced by Millar McCowan (those lovely Scottish folk who brought us the classic Highland Toffee Bar), the original bar is a fantastically tongue-tingling raspberry with green and yellow sugar crystals. Whilst this is still incontrovertibly the Wham Bar connoisseur's Wham Bar, recent years have seen the introduction of the strawberry, cola and brew flavours (the latter tipping a culinary hat to a certain soft drink manufactured north of the border) with sours also appearing on newsagents' shelves.

Like its toffee counterpart, the Wham Bar has undergone some subtle changes over the years. The latest bar is thinner and softer than the 1980s original and no longer threatens to shatter or lever out your front teeth when bitten. The packaging has also changed and we are no longer treated to the wonderfully enlightening facts about planetary motion and orbiting satellites that once graced the reverse and somehow made the whole process of eating a Wham Bar seem vaguely educational.

FACT

Wham Bars are now also available in Mini and Mega sizes – perfect for any occasion.

WHY NOT TRY...

Fizz Wiz – the ultimate fizz!

Drumstick – the longer lasting chew

WINE GUMS

Length:
22–35 mm

Width:
10–22 mm

Depth:
12 mm

Weight:
5 g

Hero-2-Zero:
27 sec
(chewed)
2 min 21 sec
(sucked)

It is a well-known fact that if you are stuck for an idea of what to buy a senior male relative at Christmas you can rarely go wrong with a big box of Wine Gums. This perennial 'dad sweet' has stood the test of time undergoing few, if any, changes in its long and esteemed existence since it was invented by Charles Gordon Maynard, son of Maynard's founder Charles Riley Maynard, in 1909. At the time of its creation, however, Maynard Snr was less than impressed. Convinced that these new sweets contained alcohol, in complete contravention of his strict Methodist and teetotal ways, he threatened to dismiss his son immediately. The Wine Gum actually contained no wine at all – its name only referred to the fact that the subtle fruit flavours were said to offer an experience similar to savouring a fine vintage. Only some frantic and frenzied explanations saved Charles Gordon Maynard his job and the rest of us the Wine Gum!

There are no special skills required in eating a Wine Gum – a fact which might well contribute to its ongoing popularity. It is, though, worth mentioning that you should always endeavour to purchase Wine Gums that are as fresh as possible – these can generally be identified by their light, slightly oily sheen. If you are offered Wine Gums that appear flat in colour or are at all hard to the touch, walk away and make your purchase elsewhere.

FACT

Burgundy, Champagne, Claret, Port and Sherry are the only words that appear on proper Wine Gums.

WHY NOT TRY...

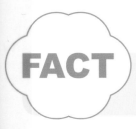 **Jelly Babies – fruity but sweeter**

 **Midget Gems – smaller and harder but yummy**

ACKNOWLEDGEMENTS

I would like to offer my thanks to the following people without whom *The Sucker's Guide* would not have been possible:

Sue King (Jelly Babies) & Julie Hawker (Sharps Mint Toffees) of Coco, 7a Fountain Street, Nailsworth, Gloucestershire, GL6 0BL, for supplying copious amounts of sweets and answering numerous questions

Sue Todd (Pontefract Cake) & Mark Todd (Aniseed Twists), for helping to inspire the project

Becky Beaves (Flying Saucers), for everything else!

Mike deHaas (Sugar Mice) of Boynes Ltd

Jason Botting (Bassetti) of www.bagsofsweets.com

Anne Muir (Galaxy Ripple) of Millar McCowan

Trevor Sharpe (Jellyatrics) of Banack Ltd

And, of course, Nicky (Cough Candy), Jennifer (Chocolate Lime) and Lucy (Wham Bar) at Summersdale for making *The Sucker's Guide* a reality.

The extract from Roy Fuller's poem 'Necrophagy' is copyright and used with the kindest permission of John Fuller (Sherbet Lemons).